Disney · PIXAR
FINDING DORY

ISBN 978-1-4950-7318-2

Wonderland Music Company, Inc. /
Pixar Music
Sis 'N Bro Music Company obo
Unforgettable Standards [U.S.A. Only]
Bourne Co. [Rest of the World]

DISTRIBUTED BY

HAL·LEONARD®

7777 W. BLUEMOUND RD. P.O. BOX 13819 MILWAUKEE, WI 53213

Visit Hal Leonard Online at www.halleonard.com

KELPCAKE

Music by
THOMAS NEWMAN

Moderately

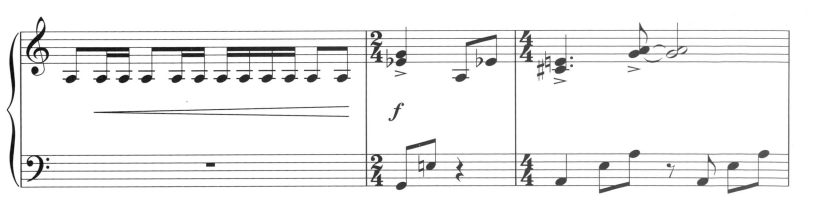

FINDING DORY
(Main Title)

Music by
THOMAS NEWMAN

Moderately, flowing

A little slower

rit.

JEWEL OF MORRO BAY

Music by
THOMAS NEWMAN

Moderately fast, in 2

Moderately slow, freely

Moderately, evenly

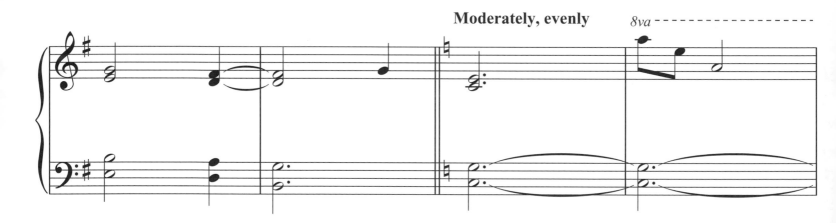

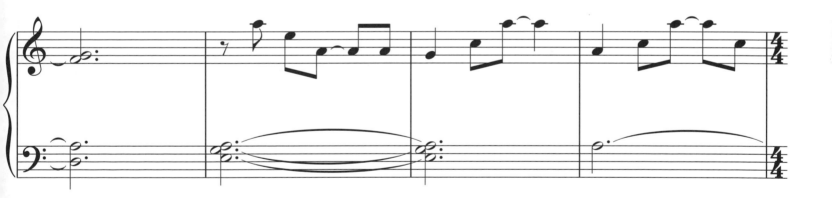

GNARLY CHOP

Music by
THOMAS NEWMAN

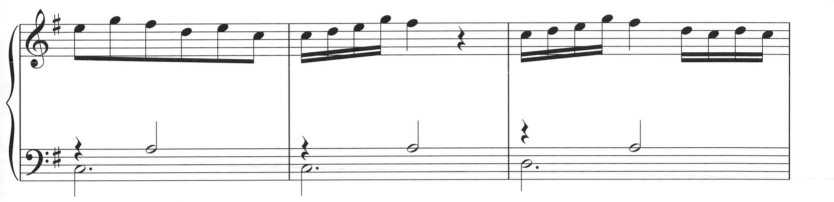

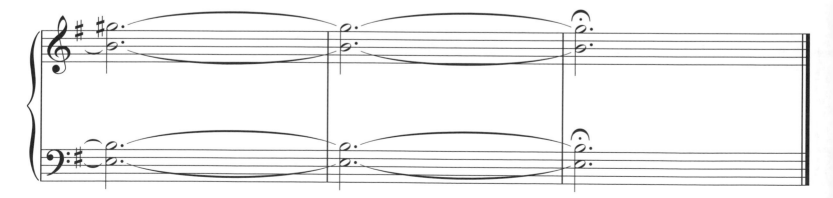

JOKER AT WORK

Music by
THOMAS NEWMAN

Moderately fast

ALMOST HOME

Music by
THOMAS NEWMAN

Moderately slow

Moderately fast, steady

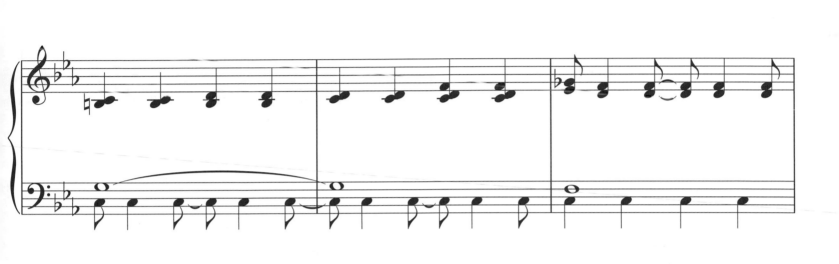

ALL ALONE

Music by
THOMAS NEWMAN

Very steady, mysterious

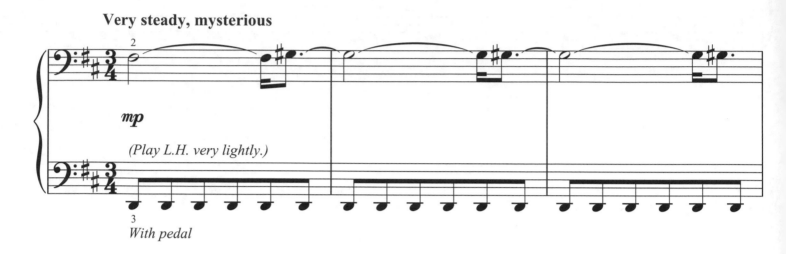

mp

(Play L.H. very lightly.)

With pedal

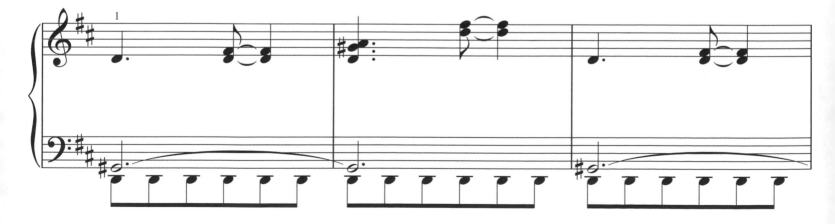

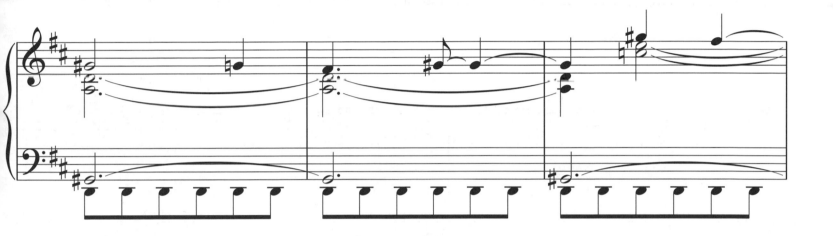

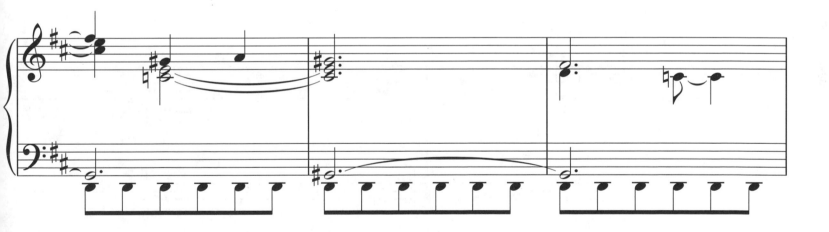

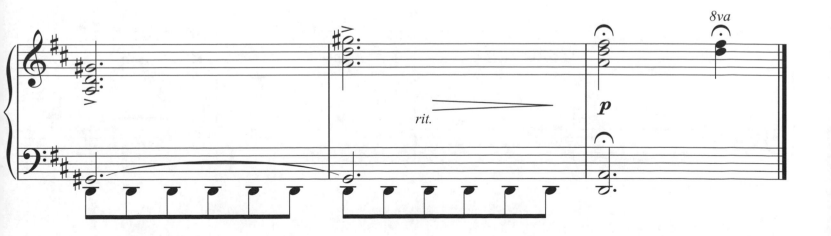

...SHELLS

Music by
THOMAS NEWMAN

Moderately, freely

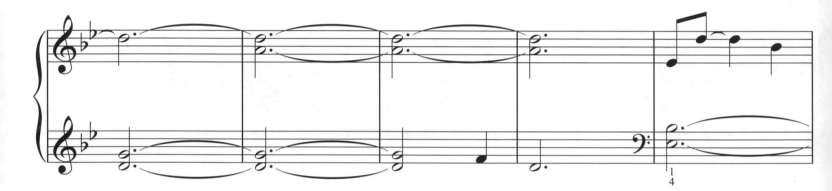

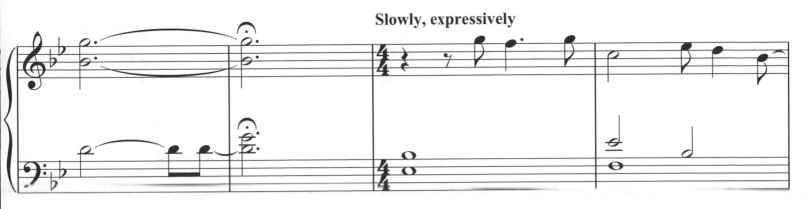

Slowly, expressively

Tempo I

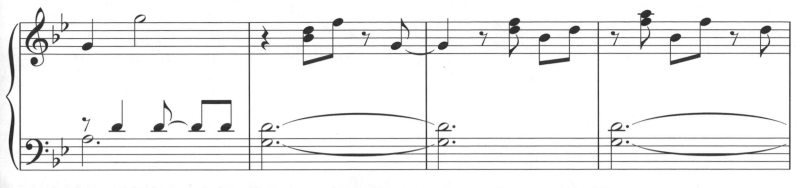

Moderately

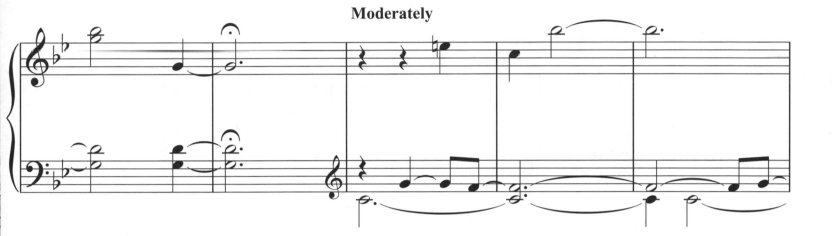

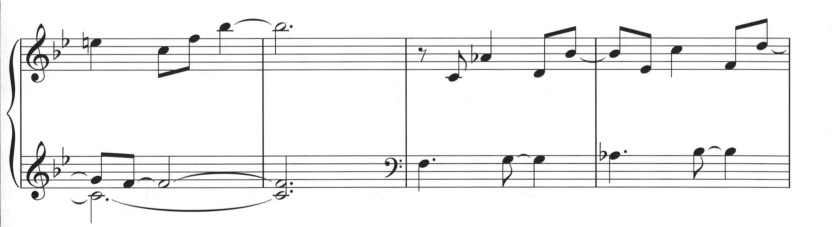

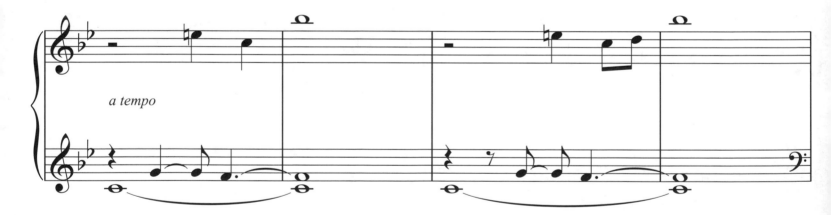

OKAY WITH CRAZY

Music by
THOMAS NEWMAN

Moderately

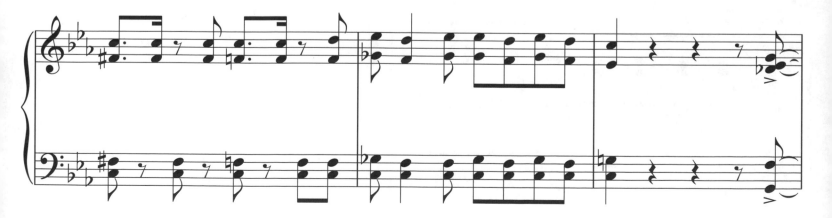

HIDE AND SEEK

Music by
THOMAS NEWMAN

QUITE A VIEW

Music by
THOMAS NEWMAN

Moderately slow, expressively

With pedal

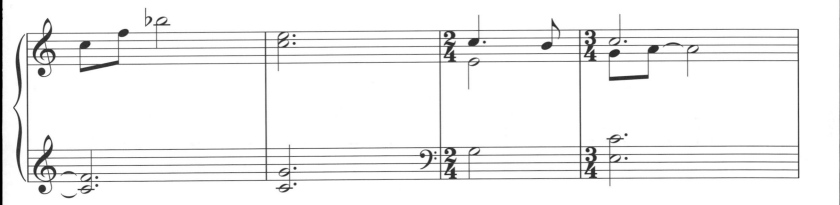

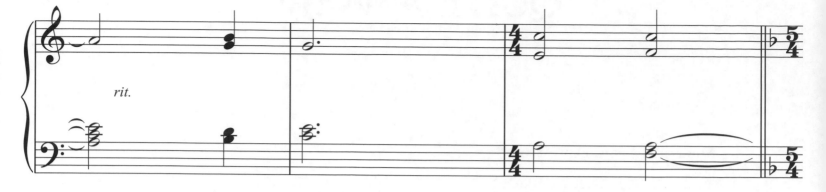

Moderately, flowing

A little slower

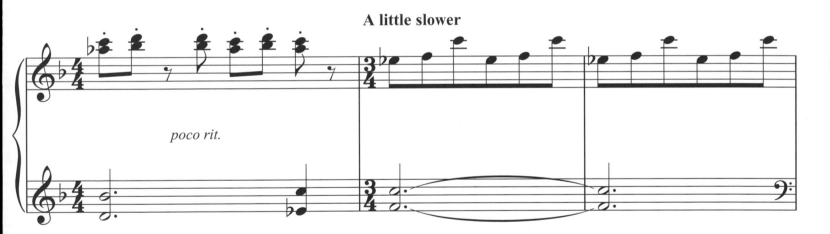

poco rit.

8va

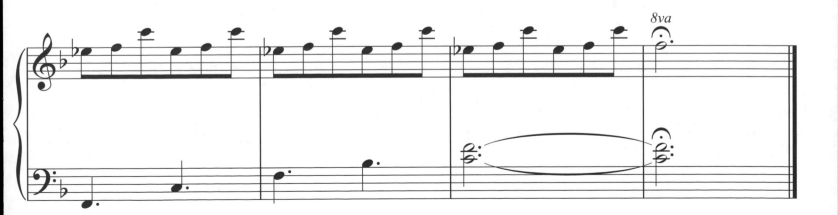

UNFORGETTABLE

Words and Music by
IRVING GORDON

Moderate Ballad

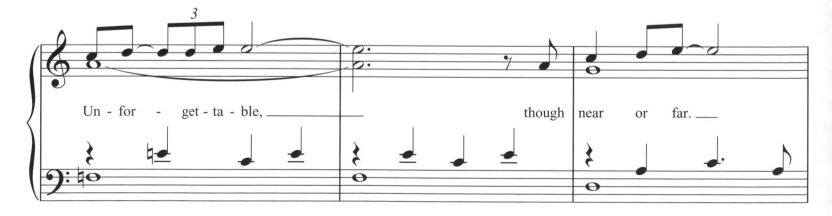

Like a song of love that clings to me,

how the thought of you does things to me. Nev - er be -

fore has some-one been more

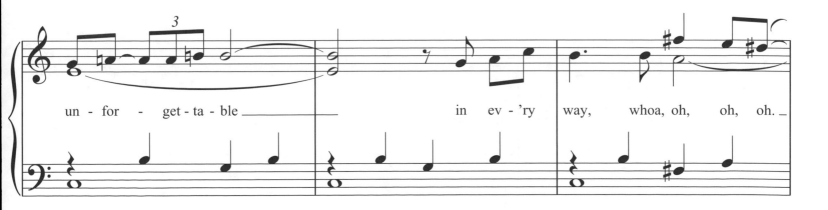

un - for - get - ta - ble in ev - 'ry way, whoa, oh, oh, oh.

And for - ev - er - more _____ that's how _____

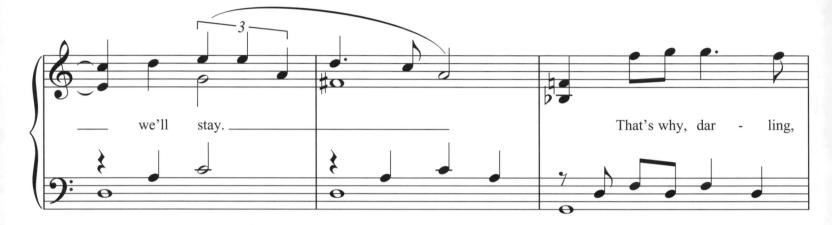

_____ we'll stay. _____ That's why, dar - ling,

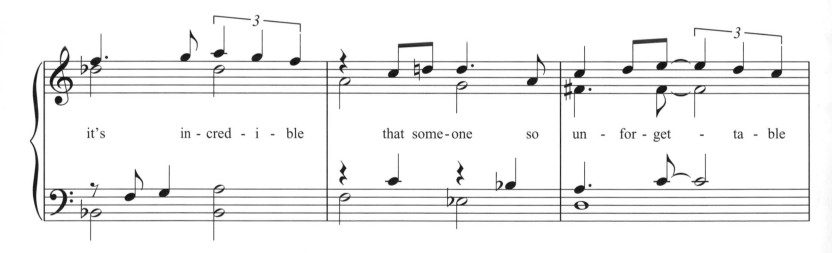

it's in - cred - i - ble that some - one so un - for - get - ta - ble

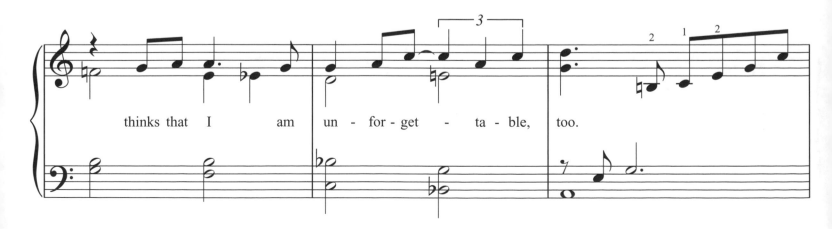

thinks that I am un - for - get - ta - ble, too.

That's why, dar - ling, it's in - cred - i - ble

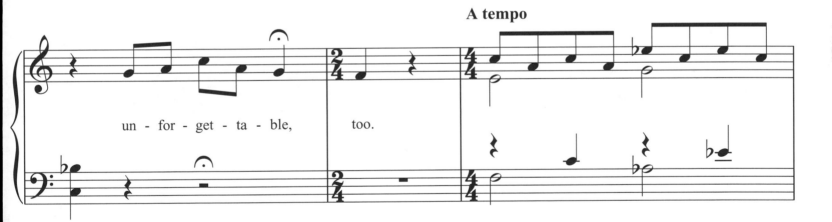

that some - one so un - for - get - ta - ble thinks that I am

rit.

A tempo

un - for - get - ta - ble, too.

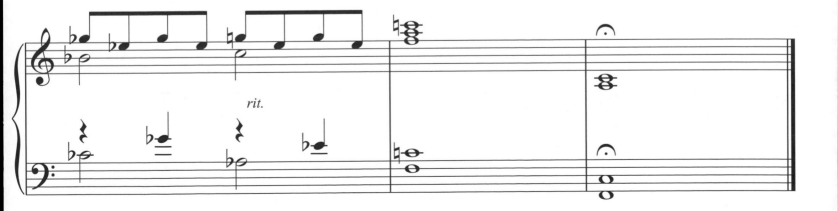

rit.

THREE HEARTS
(End Title)

Music by
THOMAS NEWMAN

Moderately

LOON TUNE

Music by
THOMAS NEWMAN

Moderately fast

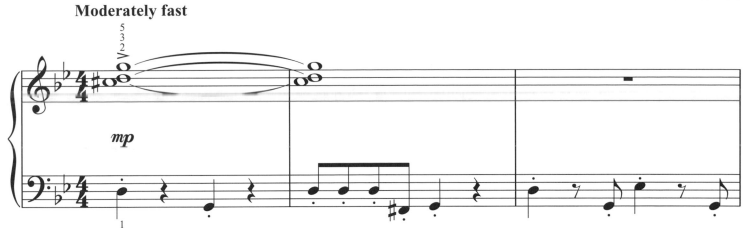

WHAT A WONDERFUL WORLD

Words and Music by GEORGE DAVID WEISS
and BOB THIELE

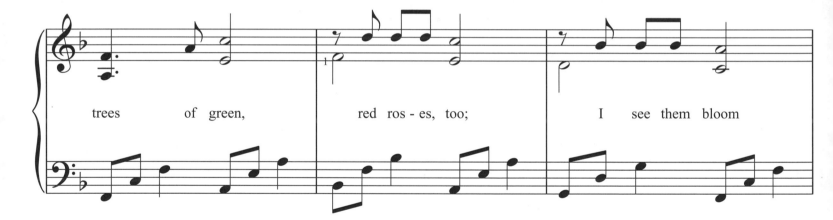

"What a won-der-ful world." I see

skies of blue and clouds of white, the bright ___ bless-ed day, the

dark ___ sa-cred night, ___ and I think ___ to my-self,

"What a won-der-ful world." The

col - ors of the rain - bow, so pret - ty in the sky, are

al - so on the fac - es of peo - ple go - in' by. I see

friends shak - in' hands, say - in', "How do you do?"

They're real - ly say - in', "I love you." I hear ba - bies cry, I

rit.   *a tempo*

watch them grow. They'll learn much more than

I'll _____ ev - er know, _____ and I think _____ to my - self,

"What a won - der - ful world." _____ Yes, I

think to my - self, "What a won - der - ful world." _____

rit.

FISH WHO WANDER

Music by
THOMAS NEWMAN

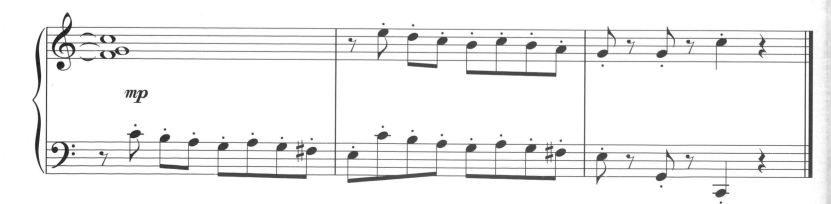